RWE Tower Dortmund Gerber Architekten

Text: Olaf Winkler
Fotografien/Photographs: Hans Jürgen Landes

JUNIUS

5	Ästhetischer Pragmatismus Der RWE Tower in Dortmund als städtisches Element
12	Aesthetic Pragmatism The RWE Tower in Dortmund: An Element in the Urban Texture
20	Der RWE Tower/The RWE Tower
63	Zeichnungen/Drawings
68	Klarheit und Komplexität Die Bauten von Professor Eckhard Gerber, Gerber Architekten, Dortmund
69	Clarity and Complexity The Work of Professor Eckhard Gerber, Gerber Architekten, Dortmund/Germany
77	Anhang/Appendix

Ästhetischer Pragmatismus
Der RWE Tower in Dortmund als städtisches Element

Drei Hochhäuser ragen im Norden der Dortmunder Innenstadt dicht beieinander in den Himmel, zwei von ihnen – die scharf umrissenen Quader des Sparkasse- und des so genannten IWO-Hochhauses – seit knapp vier Jahrzehnten. In ihre Mitte ist jüngst ein schwarz glänzender Turm getreten, der die beiden noch überragt: der RWE Tower, in dem von nun an die Hauptverwaltung der RWE Westfalen-Weser-Ems AG residieren wird. Eine selbstverständliche Bautengruppe ist entstanden, die den Eindruck erweckt, der Ort sei zuvor schlicht unvollendet gewesen. Wer am Dortmunder Hauptbahnhof die Ringstraße, die hier Königswall heißt, nach Osten geht, wird allerdings vor sich zunächst einer anderen architektonischen Komposition gewahr. Durch den Rhythmus des Schritts dynamisiert und in eine innere Bewegung versetzt, erinnert sie reduziert an jenes Dampfermotiv, wie es in der klassischen Moderne prägendes Zeichen des Aufbruchs war. Nur fehlen hier im Detail fast alle entsprechenden Insignien, insbesondere das strahlende Weiß, das den maritimen Eindruck meist stützte. Die scheinbar gerichtete Kraft erwächst vielmehr aus dem Zusammenspiel der drei klaren Körper selbst, die aus dieser Perspektive beieinander stehen: dem gestreckten Quader und dem dunklen gläsernen Halbrund, die Mario Botta vor wenigen Jahren zur neuen Stadt- und Landesbibliothek fügte – und eben der dahinter aufragenden gekurvten Front des RWE Towers. Als dichtes, wohl gefügtes Ensemble lässt sich auch diese Konstellation lesen; der neue Turm antwortet dem Schwung der niedrigeren Halbrotunde und modelliert mit ihr gemeinsam den Fluss des Raums vom Bahnhof Richtung Markt und zum kommerziellen Zentrum der Stadt. Und schließlich zeigt sich auch dem Passanten, der aus dem innersten Stadtkern zurückkehrt, etwa vom neuen Konzerthaus ein wenig weiter östlich, früh dieselbe weit hinaufreichende, straffe Fassade des neuen Bauwerks; diesmal weniger vorwärts drängend, eher als Prospekt. Dann schieben sich, je näher man herantritt, kleinere Bauten in den Blick, während sich der Weg auf Höhe des Museums für Kunst- und Kulturgeschichte zum engen Durchlass verjüngt. Wenn er sich wieder weitet, ist der RWE Tower nah herangerückt, am neu formulierten Platz von Amiens wird sein Umriss zur leitenden Raumbegrenzung und hat die fernwirkende Flächigkeit gegen den Maßstab des engen Stadtraums eingetauscht.

Haus im Kontext
Der Entwurf des RWE Towers stammt vom Dortmunder Architekten Eckhard Gerber, der neben den Gleisen am Bahnhofsausgang ein knappes Jahrzehnt zuvor mit dem Gebäude des Harenberg Verlags bereits ein reduziertes, einprägsames Zeichen plante. Nur wenige hundert Meter entfernt von jenem Bau, dessen markanter schlanker und gleichmäßig gerasterter Quader längs zum festen Bilderbestand der Stadt gehört, hat die Dortmunder City mit dem fast 100 Meter hohen Turm nun eine neue Landmarke bekommen. Tatsächlich handelt es sich um das nunmehr höchste Bürogebäude der Stadt, und auch dafür hat Gerber eine klare, fast strenge Form gefunden. Auf linsenförmigem Grundriss über flachem Sockel straff 22 Geschosse in die Höhe geführt und mit einem souveränen Stirnbogen zum Abschluss gebracht, besitzt der Baukörper Eigenständigkeit; er erhebt sich nicht nur über seine Umgebung einschließlich der beiden älteren Hochhäuser, sondern tut dies auch ohne falsche Schüchternheit. Doch unerheblich, auf welchem Weg man sich dem RWE Tower nähert – nie ist es eitle Vereinzelung, die die Wirkung des Bauwerks dominiert. Und obwohl das Gebäude selbstverständlich von weit entfernten Orten sichtbar ist, scheint es auch darum nur nachrangig zu gehen; prägend ist stattdessen der Eindruck von Verdichtung und Überlagerung, von Modellierung städtischen Raums: Selbstbewusst tritt der Entwurf mit seiner Umgebung in Beziehung und reicht so Qualitäten an den Standort zurück, von dem er selbst profitiert.

Blick von Südosten über die Innenstadt mit dem Hochhaus-Ensemble um den RWE Tower

South-eastern view of the city with the high-rise ensemble surrounding the RWE Tower

Die Potentiale dieses Areals samt seiner Umgebung, die lange Zeit als glücklos angesehen werden musste, kamen generell erst in den letzten Jahren durch verschiedene bauliche Eingriffe zur Entfaltung – ein Prozess, in dem die Errichtung des RWE Towers keinesfalls den einzigen, aber einen weiteren wichtigen Schritt zur moderaten Neuordnung der Dortmunder Innenstadt im Ganzen sowie ihres nördlichen Randes im Besonderen darstellt. Geprägt wird die Lage vom Erbe des Wiederaufbaus, der nach einer nahezu vollständigen Zerstörung der Innenstadt nicht nur deren Neu-Bestückung mit Hochbauten, sondern vor allem deren räumliche Konfiguration bestimmte. Wer Schwarzpläne der Vor- und der Nachkriegszeit vergleicht, wird vor allem den gewachsenen Weißanteil zur Kenntnis nehmen: Wie andernorts auch, wurde die massive Zerstörung damals als Chance erkannt, sich stellenweise radikal dem neuen Leitbild einer autogerechten Stadt anzunähern. Die im Grundriss bis heute ablesbare mittelalterliche Kernstadt wurde der Ost-West-Länge nach von einer, quer dazu von zwei deutlichen Schneisen durchzogen; die dem einstigen Wall folgende Ringstraße wurde offensiv ausgebaut. Als lineares Zentrum bildete sich, südlich der Ost-West-Achse Kampstraße, der einstige Hellweg als eine der ersten Fußgängerzonen Deutschlands heraus. Der Platz von Amiens, an dem sich der RWE Tower nun erhebt, liegt gerade zwischen diesen Adern, wenige Meter nördlich der Kampstraße, ebenso nah am Burgwall, an dem heute diverse städtische Ämter ihren Sitz haben. Ausschlaggebend für den künftigen Charakter des Platzes sind jedoch insbesondere zwei Entscheidungen, die die Gewichtung dieser Setzungen nachdrücklich modifizieren: Das seit den 80er Jahren auch vor dem Hintergrund des Strukturwandels entwickelte und zuletzt 1999 neu justierte »City-Konzept« verlagert zum einen den Durchgangsverkehr vollständig auf den Wall. Begünstigt durch die Vollendung der unterirdischen Stadtbahn soll die Kampstraße nach Plänen der Düsseldorfer Architekten Fritschi Stahl Baum im zentralen Bereich zum Fußgängerboulevard umgestaltet werden. Zum anderen bilden das Harenberg-Hochhaus im Westen und die Bibliothek gerade gegenüber dem Bahnhofseingang erste wichtige Maßnahmen, um der weiten Verkehrs- und Parkplatzfläche vor dem Hauptbahnhof – die *Die Zeit* in den 90ern noch als »entschlossen reizlos« charakterisierte, die aber für den Bahnreisenden nicht weniger als das Entree zur Stadt darstellt – eine neue gestalterische Fassung und funktionale Ausrichtung zu geben. Bis auf wenige Meter reicht diese Fläche an den RWE Tower heran, um sich dort in die verschiedenen Wege gen Süden aufzuteilen. Mit dem geplanten, viel diskutierten Umbau des Bahnhofs zum »Multi-Themen-Center« soll sich die Neudefinition dieses Areals als städtischer Schwerpunkt und als Brückenschlag zur hinter den Gleisen anschließenden Nordstadt fortsetzen.

Logik und Form
Das Grundstück des RWE Towers hat sich damit mehr denn je ins Zentrum wichtigster Verbindungen verlagert, die darüber hinaus nicht mehr an die Hauptverkehrsachsen gebunden sind, sondern ein differenziertes Fußwegenetz respektieren. Der Neubau reagiert nicht nur darauf, sondern gestaltet vor allem durch die konkrete Ausbildung der Erdgeschosszone dieses Wegenetz dezidiert mit und überträgt im Ganzen das vorgegebene, nahezu monofunktionale Programm in urbane Wirksamkeit. Eckhard Gerber erhielt den Planungsauftrag von Seiten der Dortmunder DIAG GmbH & Co. KG II als Investorin, bevor der spätere Mieter feststand. Verlangt war demnach zunächst ein zweckmäßiger und flexibel markttauglicher Bürobau; der Entwurf reagiert darauf mit einem entsprechenden Pragmatismus, der zugleich der generellen rationalen Haltung des Gerberschen Arbeitens folgt.

Nachdem das City-Konzept der Stadt an diesem Standort einen Turm auf quadratischem Grundriss imaginierte, ergaben sich der nun ausgeführte linsenförmige Umriss und seine aus der Straßenflucht gedrehte Position durch die exakte Analyse von zur Verfügung stehender Fläche und Zweck.

Der Entwurf verbindet auf diese Weise die Vorteile eines gestreckten Zweibünders mit denen eines kompakten, konzentrisch angelegten Grundrisses: Während die Notwendigkeit, zwei Fluchttreppenhäuser vorzuhalten, in Kombination mit Fluchtweglängen und arbeitsplatzgerechten Belichtungstiefen einen länglichen Grundriss nahe legt, wie er typologisch insbesondere im rechtwinklig umgrenzten Scheibenhochhaus seine Ausformung gefunden hat, nimmt der zentrale Kern sämtliche Elemente der Infrastruktur – fünf Aufzüge, Treppen, Nebenräume und Schächte – auf und hält so die Fassade vollständig für die Anordnung von Büroflächen frei. Die Linsenform optimiert diese Balance auch gegenüber einer vergleichbaren Ellipse, weil die Einzelräume annähernd orthogonale Zuschnitte erhalten und insbesondere an den Kopfenden nicht radial begrenzte, sondern nahezu quadratische Flächen entstehen. Formal greift der RWE Tower damit auf einen bewährten Typus zurück, wie er jüngst etwa auch für den Frankfurter Millenium Tower von Albert Speer & Partner gewählt wurde. Konstruktiv verbindet sich beim RWE Tower der statisch wirksame Kern mit in die Fassade gesetzten Stahlbetonstützen; zudem konnte (durch Einbau einer Sprinkleranlage) die zusammenhängende Nutzfläche mit einer üppigen lichten Raumhöhe von knapp drei Metern als ein Brandabschnitt deklariert werden. Beides erlaubt eine freie Einteilung vom einfachen Zellenbüro bis zum Großraum oder deren beliebige Kombination etwa für Sondergeschosse, zu denen in der konkreten Realisierung beispielsweise die Vorstandsräume im 19. und der Konferenz- und Schulungsbereich im 20. Obergeschoss zählen. In Relation zu diesen konstruktiven Bedingungen wurde die äußere Haut als gleichmäßige, klimatechnisch umsichtig gestaltete Lochfassade in die Höhe geführt. Eine grundsätzliche Bauhöhe von rund 100 Metern ergab sich aus den Abstandsflächen in Abstimmung mit den Nachbarn und wurde später den Ansprüchen des Nutzers gemäß auf 91 Meter reine Gebäudehöhe zuzüglich der Antenne spezifiziert.

Es ist die besondere Qualität des Entwurfs, dass Gerber das derart rational entwickelte Volumen mit einer Bruttogeschossfläche von 27 300 Quadratmetern mittels weniger, klarer Entscheidungen und der ihm eigenen logischen Architektursprache in eine überzeugende und städtisch wirksame Form zu verwandeln weiß. Herausragende Bedeutung kommt dabei der Detaillierung der Fassade zu, bei der die zu öffnenden Einzelfenster ebenso wie die mit silbergrauen Blechen verhüllten Brüstungen hinter die äußere Ebene zurückgenommen sind. An ihrer statt bildet eine rahmenlose Prallscheibe den äußeren Abschluss, zurückversetzt lediglich um die Stärke des polierten schwarzen Granits, der für die Verkleidung der Geschossdecken und Stützen ausgewählt wurde. Zugleich ist das Verhältnis offener und geschlossener Anteile derart balanciert, dass sich statt des Eindrucks einer klassischen Lochfassade mit ihrer punktuell durchbrochenen Massivität vielmehr das Bild einer dünnen, durch gleichmäßige Perforation bestimmten Gitterstruktur einstellt.

Überraschenderweise ist es gerade die hochglänzende Schwärze des polierten Granits, in der sich beim Blick aufwärts der Himmel und die umgebende Bebauung spiegeln, die dieser Haut unerwartete Leichtigkeit verleiht. Gestützt wird dieser Eindruck dadurch, dass die Perforation nicht bis zu den Kanten der Hauptansichten durchläuft, sondern von einem schmalen Rand umrahmt wird, und durch die Ausbildung der schmalen Fronten als vertikale Glasfugen. Nachts als bläuliche Lichtbänder inszeniert, lassen letztere das Gebäude endgültig nicht mehr als lastenden Körper erscheinen, sondern als ein Paar zueinander gestellte, durch die Eigenkrümmung stabilisierte Schalen, deren Materialstärke nur jener der Natursteinschicht zu entsprechen scheint. Mehr noch lässt Gerber diese klare geometrische Fügung am oberen Ende nicht einfach ins Leere laufen: Statt durch ein Flachdach werden die beiden Schalen durch zwei schräge Schnitte, der eine steiler, der andere flacher angesetzt, zu einem jeweils bogenförmigen Abschluss gebracht. Die steilere der beiden Schnittflächen ist als nahezu unprofiliertes Glasdach ausgebildet, über dem an diesigen Abenden ein Lichtschleier steht; in der Fernwirkung erscheint derweil wiederum nur die Schale als materielles Element. Ohne sich einer großen Geste zu bemühen, erlangt das Gebäude durch diesen einfachen formalen Kniff eine Zeichenhaftigkeit, die zugleich am Kopf des Gebäudes eine erstaunliche räumliche Großzügigkeit generiert. Von außen ablesbar auch durch die ansteigende Höhe der Fenster, hat der Architekt hinter dem höheren Stirnbogen einen weiten, lichtdurchfluteten Raum geschaffen, der sich im großzügigen Schwung über die gesamte Breite des Gebäudes erstreckt und eine maximale Höhe von 17 Metern erreicht. Umso bemerkenswerter ist, dass sich hinter den überschlanken Fenstern kein exklusiver Bereich für den Vorstand verbirgt, sondern mit dem Kasino ein allen im Hause Beschäftigten zugänglicher, quasi-öffentlicher Ort.

Organische Vermittlung
Die gleiche rationale Haltung, die an der Gebäudeform im Großen ablesbar ist, bestimmt denn auch die kleinräumliche Modellierung des städtischen Kontexts – mit einem verwandten, aber entsprechend eigenen Regeln folgenden Ergebnis. Inhaltlich ist dies der Ort, an dem die Monofunktion des Gebäudes aufgebrochen wird und sich neben dem Foyer zum Stadtraum orientierte Ladenlokale einfinden. Gerbers Bau rekurriert dabei auf den Typus eines stereometrischen Körpers über einem ausgreifenden, städtebaulich wirksamen Sockel, wie er insbesondere in Gordon Bunshafts Lever House in New York 1952 seinen Prototyp gefunden hat. Im gleichen Maße, wie sich der Entwurf darauf bezieht, setzt er sich jedoch davon ab: Es ist die Figur als Ganzes, aus der heraus Gerber diese Sockel-

zone entwickelt, ohne dem Turm additiv einen vermittelnden Körper, gleichsam eine Plinthe, unterschieben zu müssen. Das Gebäude selbst, als Objekt, weitet sich aus und greift auf zurückhaltende Weise Raum, ein Effekt, der die Rundung der Fassade als Voraussetzung nutzt. Die Materialität des Gesamtbaus setzt sich ungebrochen in die Erdgeschosszone fort und signalisiert Einheit; das Fenstermaß bewahrt Proportion, wurde bei größerer Geschosshöhe allerdings auf zwei Achsen verdoppelt, so dass der Baukörper aufgeständert erscheint. Der Umriss entspricht derweil entlang des Platzes von Amiens und rund um die nordwestliche Spitze des Gebäudes den darüber aufsteigenden Fassaden. Erst dann verlässt er – ein im Übrigen heikler, doch sorgfältig gelöster Detaillierungspunkt – die vorgegebene Linie und nähert sich, noch immer leicht gekurvt, der nach Süden folgenden Häuserflucht längs der Straße an. Dort bindet er die Rampe zur (vorhandenen, nun neu geplanten) Tiefgarage und eine bestehende Zulieferrampe ein und führt als Pergola aufgelöst schließlich vor den zur Platzfläche orientierten Haupteingang zurück. Der Baukörper entrollt sich, oder in umgekehrter Richtung betrachtet: dreht sich fast unmerklich ein und leitet so selbstverständlich ins Innere.

Formal ausgedrückt vollzieht sich mit der Gestaltung des Sockels der Übergang von einer geometrisch strengen zur organischen Form und zugleich eine Modifikation des Figur-Grund-Verhältnisses. Was abstrakt klingt, hat konkrete Relevanz: Der Grundriss des Erdgeschosses ist auch Ergebnis äußerer Kräfte, die von der vorhandenen Rampe und grundstücksrechtlichen Bedingungen über eingeübte wie neu zu »stimulierende« Wege bis zur gewünschten Neuformulierung des Platzes von Amiens reichen. Der ursprüngliche Platz dieses Namens erstreckte sich vom jetzigen Standort des RWE Towers über den Hinterhof der südlich angrenzenden Bebauung bis hin zur eher ungastlichen Tordurchfahrt Richtung Kampstraße. Die städtische Planung bestimmte die Verlagerung dieses Platzes nach Norden, mit Anbindung an den schmalen Durchgang, der rechts des Museums für Kunst und Kulturgeschichte nach Osten führt. Zugleich sah noch das City-Konzept von 1999 die vollständige Abschnürung der alten Platzfläche durch unmittelbares Andocken des Neubaus an seinen südlichen und seinen östlichen Nachbarn – ein »Westfalenforum« getauftes Einkaufszentrum – vor. Eigentumsrechtliche Gründe und Bestimmungen hinsichtlich der Feuerwehrzufahrten haben diese Anschlüsse verhindert, so dass die alte Platzfläche keineswegs aus dem Netz öffentlicher Räume getilgt wird. Der Entwurf für den RWE Tower begreift dies jedoch nicht als Atavismus, sondern als zusätzliche stadträumliche Qualität. Im Gegensatz zu einem vollständig eingebauten Eckturm fängt er durch die Form seines Sockels den neuen Platz von Amiens, ohne den fließenden Anschluss Richtung Bahnhof zu unterbrechen, und bietet zugleich zwei natürliche Übergänge zum rückwärtigen Raum. Letzterer wird als Passage wie als intimerer Hof definiert; was ihm zur Realisierung dieser Intimität noch fehlt, ist allerdings eine Gestaltung, die auch die heruntergekommenen Rückfronten der Nachbarbauten einschließt. Für die alte Platzfläche selbst hat Gerber im Zuge des Entwurfs einen klaren Vorschlag erarbeitet, der nun der Umsetzung harrt, und der Bebauungsplan erlaubt mittlerweile an der unattraktiven Rückseite des Westfalenforums Gastronomie mit entsprechenden Außenbereichen.

Entgegen kommt dieser Perspektive auch die Nutzung von etwa zwei Dritteln des Sockels durch Ladenlokale. Der Entwurf sieht grundsätzlich drei entsprechende Einheiten vor; auf Wunsch eines der Mieter wurden die beiden größeren verbunden und stellen nun ihrerseits einen inneren Brückenschlag von der Straße zum hinteren Außenraum dar. Spürbar wird dabei der Höhenanstieg des Geländes, der durch mehrere Stufen aufgefangen wird und so auch im Inneren einen eher fließenden Raum generiert. Das kleinere Lokal zur Straße – ein Friseur, der Gerber Architekten auch mit der Inneneinrichtung beauftragt hat – profitiert insbesondere von der sich ergebenden luxuriösen Raumhöhe. Dennoch bleibt der Sockel im Ganzen eingeschossig und schließt damit gestalterisch und inhaltlich an die pavillonartigen, ebenfalls durch Einzelhandel genutzten Vorbauten der südlich folgenden 60er-Jahre-Bebauung an: eine weitere Anknüpfung im Sinne einer Nicht-Ausschließlichkeit, die sich hier als Kennzeichen stadträumlichen Denkens erweist – und damit im Gegensatz zur Nachkriegszeit steht, in der es vor allem um ein fixierendes Kanalisieren der Bewegung ging, um ausschließende Zuweisung. Stattdessen bieten sich nun allein rund um den RWE Tower drei in ihrer räumlichen Erscheinung unterschiedliche Wege an, zu Fuß vom Bahnhof Richtung Markt oder Fußgängerzone zu gelangen: eine Bereicherung des städtischen Raums, in dem der RWE Tower nicht dominant, sondern moderat lenkend wirksam wird.

Innere Gestalt

Der RWE Tower geriert sich damit, trotz der Bedeutung und für Dortmund wirtschaftlich wichtigen Funktion seines Hauptnutzers, nicht als spektakulärer Einzelgänger, sondern als zurückhaltender Ort, der sich ohne Manierismen einer funktionalen Belegung anbietet. Entsprechend bleibt auch im Inneren diese Haltung als Grundlage zweckmäßiger und ästhetischer Entscheidungen spürbar. Schon das Pergola-artige Glasdach vor dem Haupteingang, der sich der städtebaulichen Prägung gemäß zum Platz von Amiens ausrichtet, scheint eben weniger als ostentative Geste denn konsequent aus der Formung des Sockels entwickelt. Das Foyer selbst, von diesem äußeren Vorraum ohne Windfang und nur durch einen Luftvorhang getrennt, zieht sich parallel zum Platzraum längs um den inneren Funktionskern herum und einige Stufen herab. Im ursprünglichen Entwurf war hier ein weiteres Ladenlokal vorgesehen; die RWE Westfalen-Weser-Ems AG möchte den Raum, der sich an der Spitze des

Baukörpers ergibt, für Ausstellungen und ähnliche Veranstaltungen nutzen. Zugleich eröffnet sich direkt am Empfangsdesk und einer Sicherheitsschleuse vorbei der Zugang zum zentralen Kern mit den Aufzügen. Der schwarze Granit der Fassade setzt sich derweil als spiegelnder Bodenbelag fort und tritt in scharfen Kontrast zum weißen Putz der Wände: eine Klarheit, zu der Details wie der Verzicht auf Unterzüge an den Durchgängen oder die abgerundeten Wangen der Aufzugstüren beitragen. Trotz der stofflichen Nähe zur äußeren Gestalt hat der Innenraum eine delikatere Fügung erhalten; das Foyer ist davon geprägt, bewahrt zugleich aber noch etwas vom Außenraumcharakter.

Erfreulicherweise sind Bauherr und RWE Westfalen-Weser-Ems AG auch im Weiteren dem Farbkonzept Gerbers gefolgt, das ganz auf die zurückhaltende Eleganz von Schwarz- und dunklen Grau- bis hin zu Weißtönen setzt. Diese Haltung korrespondiert mit der Reduktion der Materialien; sie ist indes Charakterzug des Gerberschen Werks. Die entsprechende Farbgebung findet sich auch im Stallgebäude des Dortmunder »Tönnishofs«, das der Architekt zum eigenen Büro umbaute, und in den meisten Projekten wieder, oft kontrastiert durch wenige Töne einer wärmeren Palette. Im RWE Tower sind reinweiß die Decken und Wände, anthrazit die offenen Teeküchen, die sich in jeder Etage an den Spitzen des inneren Kerns befinden, die Teppichböden und die Stahlzargen der mit einer transluzenten Folie beschichteten Glastüren. Deren milchiges Weiß bestimmt auch die weiten Glastrennwände im Konferenz- und Schulungsbereich im 20. Obergeschoss, während die RWE Westfalen-Weser-Ems AG sich in den Standardgeschossen für geschlossene Trennwände entschied. Obwohl der Bezug des innen liegenden Flurs nach außen so stärker eingeschränkt wird, als es innerhalb der flexibel und großzügig unterteilbar angelegten Bürobereiche notwendig gewesen wäre, öffnen die transluzenten Glastüren die Flure zum Tageslicht, so dass diese tagsüber ohne künstliches Licht auskommen. Auf der Vorstandsetage konnten vor den Aufzügen offene Bereiche eingeräumt werden; in diesem wie im Konferenzgeschoss zeichnet Gerber darüber hinaus auch für die Ausstattung verantwortlich und überführt so die entwerferische Linie in ein formal und farblich entsprechend zurückgenommenes Mobiliar.

Umso bewusster setzen Architektur und Farbgebung schließlich dort, wo sich das Gebäude an seiner obersten Spitze im Wortsinne entfaltet, einen kraftvollen Kontrapunkt: Auch der weite Raum des Kasinos wurde samt Einrichtung als Einheit entworfen; in kräftigem Orangerot leuchten dabei die Tresen des offenen Küchenbereichs und der Teppich auf der im weiten Schwung geführten Ebene und der Empore. Letztere wurde längs des inneren Kerns als Stahlfiligran eingezogen und verleiht dem hohen Halbrund nachdrücklich eine dritte Dimension. Ausschlaggebend für den erhebenden Eindruck aber ist vor allem das makellose Glasdach, das sich darüber erstreckt und im Verbund mit den hohen Fenstern üppiges Licht hereinholt. Das Gefühl gleicht fast dem, in einem Außenraum zu stehen; dass die Schrägstellung der Glasfläche nebenbei etwa die Konstruktionen zur Entwässerung minimierte, kommt unmittelbar der atmosphärischen Klarheit zu Gute. Bestechend unaufwendig überspannen schlanke Träger den weiten Raum und scheinen sich, eingeschlagen in Spiegelbleche, vollständig zu entmaterialisieren. Nicht einmal Sonnenschutzmaßnahmen stören das Bild, stattdessen genügen auf der nach Nordosten gerichteten Dachfläche einfache aufgedruckte, schwarze »Dots«, die für das Auge unsichtbar bleiben. Der Blick hinauf findet nichts als Himmel und Wolken; jener durch die Fenster wandert über das atemberaubende Panorama der Stadt.

Nachhaltigkeit als konstruktives Konzept
Die klare Gestalt des Glasdaches, die sich ganz in den Dienst der räumlichen Wahrnehmung stellt, fügt sich in Gerbers verblüffend nahe liegenden, bewusst auf Reduktion setzenden Umgang mit (klima-)technischen Fragen überhaupt. Mehr noch ist davon selbstredend die vertikale Hülle betroffen und damit die ökologisch umsichtige Erzeugung eines angenehmen Raumklimas, die gemeinhin den im Betrieb anfallenden Energiebedarf maßgeblich bestimmt. Wie kaum ein anderes ist dieses Thema in den Vordergrund getreten, seit sich in den »autistischen Kisten« der 50er und 60er Jahre mit ihrer Einfachverglasung das Sick Building Syndrom breit machte und Tauwasser bis hin zur Eiszapfenbildung die Bauphysik ruinierte. Dass Vollklimatisierung überholt ist und individuell zu öffnende Fenster zum zumindest wünschenswerten Standard im Hochhausbau gehören, ist demnach profan. Die technologische Entwicklung – und die öffentliche Wahrnehmung – hat sich allerdings insbesondere auf die aufwendige und kostenträchtige Realisierbarkeit dieser Ansprüche bei möglichst volltransparenten Hochbauten konzentriert. Die Lochfassade des RWE Towers reduziert stattdessen den Anteil der Glasflächen erheblich und schützt das Gebäude so von vornherein konstruktiv vor Überhitzung ebenso wie vor übermäßiger Auskühlung; zugleich ergänzt die Ausbildung der Fensteröffnungen dies um die Vorteile einer zweischaligen Hülle mit durchlüftetem Zwischenraum. Innen wurden individuell zu öffnende Flügel mit Doppelverglasung angeordnet, die äußere Ebene bildet eine einfache Prallscheibe mit horizontalen Schlitzen am oberen und unteren Ende. Sie schützt bei geöffnetem Fenster vor übermäßigem Winddruck und umschließt einen im Zwischenraum liegenden Sonnenschutz aus Metall-Lamellen, die im hochgefahrenen Zustand vollständig verborgen bleiben. Als Blendschutz dienen beschichtete Textilbahnen auf der Rauminnenseite. Die klimatischen Bedingungen lassen sich somit individuell und mittels natürlicher Belüftung regeln. Nur zu Spitzenzeiten treten unterstützend unter den Fenstern angebrachte Einzelheizkörper bzw. eine Kühlung über das Ein-

bringen von konditionierter Luft und eine Betonkernaktivierung hinzu; in zwei Geschossen ist eine Kühldecke eingebracht.

Das Gebäude erlangt auf diese Weise eine energetische Nachhaltigkeit, die sich gerade im alltäglichen Betrieb unmittelbar in einem minimierten, an den unteren Werten jüngster gesetzlicher Verordnungen orientierenden Energieaufwand ausdrückt. Die angesichts des Bautypus ungewohnte technologische Disziplinierung ist dafür Grundlage und innerhalb der umfassenden Konzeption zugleich logischer Schluss. Einzelaspekte wie rekuperative bzw. regenerative Wärmerückgewinnung, eine auf Niedertemperaturbetrieb ausgelegte, an das Fernwärmenetz angeschlossene Heizungsanlage oder der umsichtige Einsatz konstruktiver Speichermassen werden nicht separat, sondern als funktionale, wechselwirksame Elemente des Gesamtentwurfs betrachtet. So wie die Wahl der Lochfassade gleichermaßen als Bedingung wie als Konsequenz des statisch-räumlichen Systems gelesen werden kann, stellt sich das Verhältnis zwischen Klimatechnik und Konstruktion im Ganzen als schlüssiges Gefüge dar, um die räumliche Qualität und Flexibilität zu erhöhen und zugleich bei grundsätzlich optimierten raumklimatischen Bedingungen deren individuelle Regelbarkeit zu maximieren. Im Einzelnen werden die Entscheidungen in Dortmund auch durch wirtschaftliche Gründe gestützt, die angesichts der maximal erreichbaren Gewerbemieten und bei einem Gebäude, das nicht primär als Vorzeigeobjekt einer Corporate Identity geplant wurde, dem Machbaren eine Grenze setzen. Statt dies jedoch als Einschränkung seiner entwerferischen Mittel zu verstehen, antwortet der Architekt mit einem ganzheitlichen Entwurf, der nicht wie manches Glashaus über komplexe Fassadentechnologie lösen muss, was es sich an Problemen etwa der Aufheizung und Auskühlung selbst auflädt. Der Architekt Helmut Jahn, der als Vertreter einer hoch entwickelten Glasarchitektur gelten kann, hat darauf hingewiesen, dass »das absolut ökologischste Gebäude« eines sei, »das überhaupt keine Haustechnik benötigt«. Dass dies auch der RWE Tower nicht erreichen kann, steht außer Frage; mit der Besinnung auf die Tugenden einer eher »konservativen«, der Qualität von Masse und wohl balancierter Raumöffnung bewussten Typologie, wie sie hier nicht von ungefähr am Hauptsitz eines Energie- und Wasserversorgers demonstriert wird, wird sich jeder in diese Richtung gehende Ansatz aber auseinander setzen müssen.

Durchdringung
Umso wichtiger bleibt zu bemerken, dass es sich auch dabei keinesfalls um eine dogmatische Haltung des Architekten handelt. Aus Gerbers Büro sind bereits – bei entsprechendem Kontext und Budget – bemerkenswerte Entwürfe für vollständig gläserne Hochhäuser hervorgegangen. Dazu zählt etwa der Wettbewerbsbeitrag für die Twin Towers im chinesischen Qingdao (2003), der aufgrund des kulturellen Kontextes und der mit der Ausschreibung verbundenen Ziele vollständig anderen Parametern folgt. Ausschlaggebender Grundzug bleibt vielmehr der Grad der Durchdringung, der das Detail an das »große Ganze« knüpft und bei allem Pragmatismus explizit gestalterische Entscheidungen verlangt. Gerade durch dieses Originäre wird auf unsentimentale Weise eine Relation zum Ort hergestellt. Exempel dafür ist beim RWE Tower etwa, dass sich die exakten Fensterzuschnitte außen, vor der zurückversetzten Brüstung, keineswegs durch statische und klimatechnische Bedingungen allein begründen lassen, sondern einer künstlerischen Zielsetzung folgen. Auffallend ist allerdings, dass in der von nüchterner Massivität geprägten Dortmunder Architektur die Rhythmisierung mittels hochrechteckiger Formate ein zeitlos vertrautes Thema darstellt, das bei so unterschiedlichen Bauten wie dem Stadthaus, der IHK oder dem C&A-Gebäude, an der konkaven Stirnfront des Museums für Kunst- und Kulturgeschichte und auch am Riegel der Bibliothek wiederkehrt. In Bottas Fall ist darin konkret ein Echo auf den Hauptbaukörper des Stadttheaters aus den 60er Jahren zu sehen, zu dessen Gesamtanlage die Bibliothek in ihrer Fügung von verschlossenem Quader und freierer gläserner Form ohnehin kompositorische Parallelen aufweist. Gerber, dessen Bau mit diesem kompositorischen Konzept nichts zu tun hat, stellt zurückhaltend und ohne nun wiederum Botta eigentlich zu zitieren, dazu eben nicht nur durch die Krümmung der schwarz glänzenden Fassade, sondern auch durch die Fensterformate eine Verwandtschaft her. Indem er offene und geschlossene Flächen ausgewogen proportioniert, nähert er sich jedoch zugleich dem Prinzip des von ihm selbst entworfenen Harenberg-Hochhauses an. Dass dort ein Quadrat als Modul dient, macht diese Parallele nur deutlicher. Selbstverständlich »interessiert« sich Eckhard Gerber im eigentlichen Sinne weder für das eine noch für das andere Format; bedeutsam ist vielmehr die Rationalität, die als Entwurfsmaxime in beiden Fällen eine nahezu abstrakte Gestalt findet und so das Gebäude aus der Stadt zugleich wieder heraushebt.

Gerade auch durch die sichtbar werdenden Differenzen zeigt der Vergleich mit dem Harenberg-Hochhaus, dass kaum die konkreten Einzelentscheidungen beim RWE Tower, wohl aber ihre Herleitungen einer grundsätzlichen Haltung im Werk des Architekten entsprechen. So hat Gerber auch beim Harenberg-Hochhaus einen einprägsamen Körper mit einer ausgreifenderen, flachen Form kombiniert, die das Verhältnis von Figur und Grund umdreht, als sie ihren Umriss unmittelbar von der gekurvten Straßenflucht gewinnt. Mit dem radikalen Zulaufen Richtung Bahnhof wird dieses »Argument« im wahrsten Sinne des Wortes auf die Spitze getrieben; ein nunmehr städtebaulicher, hier fast ironisch anmutender Pragmatismus, der eine gewisse Ähnlichkeit zum Umgang mit der vorhandenen Zulieferanfahrt am RWE Tower besitzt. Vor allem aber weisen der niedrigere Teil des Harenberg-Baus und mehr noch die gläserne Zwischenzone eine Repräsentativität des Öffentlichen auf, die der Bereitstellung dieses Gebäudeteils durch den Nutzer auch für kulturelle Veranstaltungen entspricht. Am RWE Tower fehlt diese Form der Repräsentativität, weil das entsprechende Programm fehlt: Dieses Gebäude ist ein Bürobau mit einem zum Teil kommerziell genutzten Sockel; das weiß der Bau zu veredeln, aber mehr behauptet er nicht, so dass eine gewisse, angenehme Kühle verbleibt. Selbst die Eleganz der schwarz glänzenden Fassade wäre als reiner Selbstzweck kaum denkbar; weil sie aber dem Turm gegen den Himmel einen bewusst moderaten Spiegeleffekt (man vergleiche nur die grelle, 1991 erneuerte Haut des IWO-Hauses) und durch ihre scheinbare Dünnwandigkeit eine erstaunliche Leichtigkeit verleiht, wird sie für die Gesamtwirkung – nämlich die Integration einer entsprechenden Baumasse in die Stadt – unverzichtbar.

Architektur in Relation
Nebenbei lässt sich der Entwurf für den RWE Tower schließlich auch als Kommentar zu jener Hochhausdebatte lesen, die in Deutschland immer wieder aufflammt und zugleich Züge des Zeitlosen trägt. Seit es diesen Typus gibt, wird um ihn gestritten, öffentlich und zuweilen populistisch. Schwierig scheint es, sich von generellen Ressentiments zu lösen, liegt doch im Aufragen an sich ein Anlass zur Deutung von Macht, zumal mancherorts längst spektakuläre Singularität oberste Priorität besitzt. Diskussionen etwa in München, wo per Volksentscheid die maximale Höhe auf 100 Meter fixiert wurde, oder in Köln, wo aufgrund von Hochhausplanungen der Weltkulturerbestatus des Doms in Gefahr geraten ist, reduzieren die Auseinandersetzung derweil primär auf die (durchaus bedeutsame) Frage der Stadtsilhouette, bestenfalls unter Beachtung von Sichtachsen. In Dortmund haben derlei Verkürzungen zum Glück keine Rolle gespielt, was nicht nur an der Architektur des neu errichteten Hochhauses liegt, das im internationalen Vergleich eine im Übrigen nur moderate Höhe erreicht, sondern ebenso an der Struktur und den Entwicklungsperspektiven der Stadt, in die sich das Gebäude zeichenhaft und funktional einfügt. Die Schwierigkeiten des Strukturwandels, die Dortmund umso mehr treffen mussten, als die Stadt in der Nachkriegszeit eine der wirtschaftlich stärksten im gesamten Bundesgebiet war, sind mittlerweile weitgehend überwunden und stellen sich heute als Chance dar. Wenn Manfred Sack Mitte der 80er schrieb, Dortmund als Stadt wirke »immer ein wenig, als sei ihr Bild in den letzten drei Jahrzehnten nicht geduldig, geschweige von langer Hand geplant, sondern durch immer etwas plötzliche Entscheidungen entstanden«, so war das damals eine sicherlich richtige Beobachtung; heute jedoch sind die wichtigsten Entwicklungsschwerpunkte insbesondere in der Innenstadt nicht nur benannt, sondern durch ein zugrunde liegendes Konzept miteinander verknüpft, das zunehmend auch im Baulichen spürbar wird. Bemerkenswert ist dabei, dass, abgesehen von einzelnen Ausnahmen wie dem umstrittenen Bahnhofsprojekt, diese Entwicklung auf die auch jüngste Geschichte rekurriert, statt mit ihr zu brechen, vorausgesetzt die jeweiligen Planungen können dies bis in die Realisierung hinein bewahren. Beispielhaft dafür sind die sensiblen Umplanungen von Fritschi Stahl Baum für die Kampstraße, die im unmittelbaren räumlichen Zusammenhang mit dem Platz von Amiens stehen. Zugleich offenbart sich damit als ein Zug dieser Entwicklungen eine positive Moderatheit, die man sich andernorts oft wünschen würde; eine Zurückhaltung, die den überlieferten Charakter der Stadt als Qualität erkennt.

Der RWE Tower folgt dieser Zurückhaltung. Der Bau, in dem die RWE Westfalen-Weser-Ems AG mit 700 ihrer 2700 Mitarbeiter residiert, fügt sich ein zwischen zwei bestehenden Hochhäusern; als Gruppe markieren sie einen gefestigten Verwaltungsstandort innerhalb der Innenstadt. Das Dortmunder Hochhauskonzept ergänzt diesen um weitere Hochhäuser an jenen Stellen, wo die vom Stadtkern ausgehenden Radialen den Wall kreuzen: als Stadttore, als Lesbarmachung einer vorhandenen Struktur. Ganz bewusst nimmt der RWE Tower derweil Beziehungen zu den verschiedensten Räumen und Bauten auf: zu seinen beiden älteren Nachbarn, zur Bibliothek und durch seine Ausrichtung auch zum Harenberg Verlag, räumlich zu den ihn umgebenden Plätzen und Straßen, zugleich über jene auch funktional innerhalb der Verbindung kultureller und kommerzieller Orte wie dem Konzerthaus, dem Museum für Kunst- und Kulturgeschichte, dem Bahnhof. Gerade weil diese Situation als spezifische verstanden wird, liefert der Entwurf keine allgemein gültige Antwort. Aber er präsentiert ein Modell des überzeugend Naheliegenden: ästhetisch, funktional, wirtschaftlich, individuell begünstigt nicht zuletzt durch einen Bauherrn, der für den eigenen Bestand baut und dabei qualitätvolle Architektur und deren Nachhaltigkeit als ein vorrangiges Kriterium erkennt. Das Bild der »Europäischen Stadt« zu beachten heißt nicht notwendigerweise, keine Hochhäuser zu bauen. Der Gerbersche Bau liefert in diesem Sinne einen präzisen Beitrag: Hochhäuser sind, mehr als alles andere, städtebaulich wirksame Bauten, Architektur in Relation. Daran, und niemals generell gesprochen, misst sich ihre Qualität.

Aesthetic Pragmatism
The RWE Tower in Dortmund: An Element in the Urban Texture

Three skyscrapers close to each other rise up towards the sky in the north of Dortmund's city centre. Two of them – the crisply defined rectangular Sparkasse Building and the IWO Tower – have done so for almost four decades. A glossy black skyscraper has recently been added between them, towering above both of them: the RWE Tower which will now house the headquarters of RWE Westfalen-Weser-Ems AG, one of Germany's largest regional energy and water suppliers. The resulting group of buildings now creates an ensemble which gives the impression that the site was incomplete in the past. But anyone who walks to the east along the circular road from the main railway station will initially see a different architectural composition. Seemingly set in motion by the rhythm of the pedestrian's footsteps, it is in some respects reminiscent of a steam ship, a motif which was a dominant symbol of new beginnings in the architecture of classical Modernism. However, almost all of the associated insignia are missing, especially the radiant white which often emphasised the maritime impression. Instead, the seemingly directional force arises from the interplay of the three clear structures themselves, which seem from this perspective to stand next to each other: the elongated rectangular block and the semi-circular glass structure which Mario Botta combined to form the new municipal and regional library a few years ago – and behind them the curved elevation of the RWE Tower façade. This constellation, too, can be interpreted as a concentrated and skilful combination – the new tower takes up the curvature of the lower semi-circular building, and together they model the spatial flow from the station to the market and the commercial centre of the city. And finally, when the pedestrian returns to the station from the centre of the city, for example from the new Concert Hall a little further to the east, he soon sees the same towering, tautly smoothed façade of the new building; but this time it is not so imposing, more like a calm background. Then other buildings crowd in as the pedestrian comes nearer to the tower, and the route then becomes a narrow passage next to the Museum of Art and Cultural History. When it widens out again, the walker is very close to the RWE Tower, which is now the main structure defining the edge of the open space called Platz von Amiens, fitting in with the scale of the constricted local setting instead of presenting itself in the smooth large format that is visible from a distance.

The building in the context
The design for the RWE Tower was created by the Dortmund-based architect Eckhard Gerber. Almost a decade earlier he had already created a striking reductionist landmark next to the railway station, the high-rise building of the Harenberg Publishing House. Only a few hundred metres from that building, which has become a familiar visual feature of the city with its striking slender rectangular form and the even pattern of its façade, the Dortmund city now has a new landmark, a tower building which is nearly 100 metres tall. This tower is now the tallest office building in the city, and again Gerber has selected a clear, almost austere form. The lenticular floor plan above a flat base rises up for 22 storeys with a smooth façade and is crowned by a splendid arch – this is a building with its own distinctive character; it not only soars above its surroundings, including the two older skyscrapers, but it does so without any false modesty. But whatever direction we approach the RWE Tower from, the effect of the building is never dominated by the vanity of isolation. And although the building is of course also clearly visible from a distance, this does not seem to be its primary goal. The main impression is the density and the combined contours in the urban setting. The design fits in confidently with its surroundings, giving quality to the location and at the same time benefitting from its interaction with the location.

Blick von Nordwesten
North-western view

The potential of this area and the surrounding district, which was long regarded as a neglected part of the city, has only begun to unfold as a result of a number of building projects over the last few years. In this process the RWE Tower is certainly not the only element, but it represents another important step towards a moderate reorganisation of Dortmund's inner city in general and its northern edge in particular. The location is marked by the heritage of the reconstruction of the almost completely destroyed inner city, which not only gave the city new buildings, but also shaped its spatial configuration. If we look at black and white cadastral maps from the pre-war and post-war periods, we will especially notice the increase in the amount of white. Like in many other municipalities, the massive destruction was seen as an opportunity for a radical move towards a city designed for motor vehicles. The contours of the original mediaeval city are still visible, but this area has been dissected by one line of traffic infrastructure from east to west and two routes from north to south, and the circular road following the line of the old ramparts has been systematically widened. As a linear centre to the south of the east-west road (Kampstrasse), the former ›Hellweg‹, a historical trading route in this region, became one of the first pedestrian zones in Germany. Platz von Amiens, where the RWE Tower has been built, is situated between these streets just a few metres north of Kampstrasse and just as close to the circular road, which is now the site of various municipal offices. Two decisions, however, have had a particular impact on the future character of the area and radically changed the underlying spatial concept. First of all, the ›City Concept‹, which has been developed against the background of structural changes since the 1980s and was revised in 1999, concentrates the through traffic on the circular road. After the completion of the underground rail line, the central part of Kampstrasse will now be redesigned as a pedestrian boulevard based on plans by the Düsseldorf-based architects Fritschi Stahl Baum. And secondly, the Harenberg Tower to the west and the library directly opposite the station entrance were the first important projects to give a new design and function to the wide expanse of traffic and parking space in front of the railway station – an area which the weekly newspaper *Die Zeit* described in the 1990s as being ›systematically without attraction‹, but which is in fact the first part of the city seen by rail travellers. This wide open space comes very close to the RWE Tower before the pedestrian routes to the south leading into the inner city split up into several strands. The much discussed plans to convert the station into a ›multi-theme centre‹ aim to continue the development of this space as a municipal centre and a link to the northern part of the city beyond the railway lines.

Logic and form
The site of the RWE Tower is thus all the more at the heart of the routes through the city which no longer depend entirely on the main roads, but also rely on pedestrian ›pathways‹. The new building not only reacts to this situation, the design of the ground floor interacts with these pedestrian routes and translates the defined and almost monofunctional identity of the building into the reality of the urban setting. The Dortmund-based company DIAG GmbH & Co. KG II commissioned Eckhard Gerber to design the building at a time when the tenancy agreements were still not finalised. Due to the very early binding mandate, Gerber had to design a functional office building which could be marketed flexibly. The design implemented this with a pragmatism which also reflects the general rationalist approach of Gerber's work.

The concept for the city envisaged a tower on a square base in this location, but the lenticular shape that has now been built and its position at an angle to the line of the street resulted from an exact analysis of the available space and the purpose of the building. In this way, the design combines the advantages of an elongated office block and a compact, concentric floor plan. Whereas the need to create two escape staircases, in combination with the length of the escape routes and the depth of the lighting, would suggest an elongated floor plan which is typical of elongated slab-type tower buildings, the central core in the RWE Tower contains all elements of the infrastructure – five lifts, staircases, auxiliary rooms and shafts – thus keeping the façade completely free for offices. The lenticular shape optimises this balance, even compared with an ellipse, because the individual offices are almost rectangular, and in particular because the spaces at the two ends of the building are almost square. In this way, the design of the RWE Tower follows the successful principles which were recently also used for Frankfurt's Millennium Tower, for example, designed by Albert Speer & Partners. The structural stability of the RWE Tower is provided by the load-bearing core in conjunction with the reinforced concrete columns integrated into the façade. And the use of a sprinkler system meant that the entire coherent floor space, with its generous ceiling height of almost three metres, could be declared as a single fire compartment. This permits flexible use of the space, ranging from single cell-type offices to an open-plan storey or a flexible combination of the two on special storeys – in the present use of the building, for example, this includes the executive rooms on the 19th floor and the conference and training area on the 20th floor. In relation to these structural conditions, the outer cladding rises up the building as a regular perforated façade designed to optimise the inner climatic conditions. The permitted height of about 100 metres was defined in relation to the distances around the building in consultation with its neighbours, and this was later specified, in accordance with the needs of the tenant, as a basic height of 91 metres for the building plus the aerial.

The special quality of the design lies in the fact that Gerber transformed this rationally developed building volume, with its gross floor area of 27,300 square metres, into a convincing form with a distinct urban character by means of a few clear decisions and the logic of his own architectural forms of expression. In this concept, the detailed design of the façade plays an outstanding role. The individual windows that can be opened and the parapets concealed by silver-grey metal sheeting were moved back behind the outer façade layer. The outer cladding consists of an almost frameless full-size window pane which is merely set back by the thickness of the polished black granite which was selected to cover the floor slabs and support columns. This creates an elegant, almost abstract grid in which the ›beams‹ and ›posts‹ – reflecting the primary structure – are equal in thickness. At the same time the relation between open and closed elements is balanced so that instead of giving the impression of a classical perforated façade with a massive outer surface penetrated by individual windows, it conveys the image of a slender grid structure determined by even and regular perforations.

Surprisingly, the unexpected visual lightness of the façade results from the glossy black surface of the polished granite which reflects the sky and the surrounding buildings when seen from below. This impression is enhanced by the way the perforation does not extend to the ends of the building but is enclosed by a narrow border, while vertical strip windows which act as joints seem to ascend the building. These vertical windows appear as blue bands of light at night, which overcomes the massive visual volume of the building and makes it look like a pair of shell-like structures which seem to be only as thick as the stone façade and to be stabilised merely by their curvature. To crown the building, Gerber does not simply let this clear geometrical structure end abruptly at the top. Instead of a flat roof, the two shell-like sections end in two oblique cuts, one steeper than the other, with crisply defined arches at the top of the broader sections of the façade. The steeper half of the roof consists of an almost featureless glass roof which gives off a haze of light on misty evenings. Seen from a distance, only the outer shell appears to be made of solid material. Without making any great effort, the building achieves an emblematic effect by this simple formal feature, and at the same time this gives the top of the building an astonishing sense of spatial generosity. Under the taller roof arch, which extends across the whole width of the building, the architect has created a spacious, light-flooded room. It reaches a maximum height of 17 metres, which is reflected on the outside by the greater height of the windows. Surprisingly, these excessively slender windows do not conceal an exclusive area for the management – this spacious room is used as the canteen, a room which is accessible to the whole staff.

Organic mediation
The rational approach which is expressed in the shape of the building also determines the smaller dimensions of the urban context on the ground floor – with a similar result, but a result that follows rules of its own. In content, this is the place where the building's monofunctional character is overcome and shops oriented towards the city are placed next to the foyer. In general, Gerber's building is a stereometric structure above a broader base which interacts with the urban context, an approach which was especially modelled in Gordon Bunshaft's prototypical Lever Building in New York in 1952. But even in its reference to this prototype, Gerber's building is very different: this base is developed from the main volume of the building itself without any need to add a mediating structure which would act as a plinth for the tower. The building itself spreads out and modestly claims space – an effect which directly results from the curvature of the façade. The materials used for the building as

a whole are also used for the ground floor, which gives the building a visual unity. The windows retain their proportion, but in view of the greater ceiling height of the ground floor they have been doubled to cover two axes in width, making the building appear to be raised on stilts. The ground layout of the building along Platz von Amiens and around the north-west tip of the building matches the façade which rises above the base. It is only then that it leaves the defined line – a delicate detail, but one that is meticulously solved – and, retaining a slight curvature, comes closer to the line of the buildings on the street to the south. Here it integrates the ramp of the underground car park (which already existed and now needed to be replanned) and an existing supplier entrance ramp, then it moves around the building as a separate pergola and leads back to the main entrance facing Platz von Amiens. The building unravels – or, when seen from the other direction, turns almost imperceptibly inwards – and leads into the interior.

In formal terms, the design of the base creates a transition from a strict geometrical form to an organic form, and at the same time a modification of the figure-ground relationship. What sounds very abstract is in fact very practical in its relevance: The floor layout of the ground floor is also the result of external forces such as the existing ramp, the legal constraints of established rights of way, the stimulation of new pedestrian links and the need for a new design for Platz von Amiens. The original square of this name extended from the present site of the RWE Tower through the rear courtyard of the buildings to the south to the rather unattractive gateway situation leading to Kampstrasse. The municipal planning authorities stipulated that the square should be shifted to the north and connected to the narrow passage leading east to the right of the museum. At the same time, the City Concept of 1999 still proposed that the old area of the square should be completely sealed off by joining the new building directly to its neighbours to the south and east, and that the latter should become a shopping centre called ›Westfalenforum‹. This plan was foiled by property rights and the requirements for access by the fire services, so the old square was not eradicated from the network of public spaces. The design of the RWE Tower did not interpret this as an atavism, though, but developed a new quality in the urban setting. Instead of a completely integrated corner tower, the form of the base defines the new Platz von Amiens without disrupting the flow of the pedestrian route to the station, and at the same time it offers two natural ways to reach the space at the rear of the tower. This area is now defined as a passageway with a more intimate courtyard. However, to fully implement this intimacy it still needs a design that includes the rather derelict rear façades of the neighbouring buildings. For the old square itself, Gerber created a clear proposal as part of the design; this proposal is now waiting to be implemented, and the zoning plan now permits catering outlets with the associated outdoor facilities to be created on the less attractive rear side of the ›Westfalenforum‹ existing buildings.

This idea is augmented by the fact that about two thirds of the base are used by shops. The design fundamentally envisages three such units. At the request of one tenant, the two larger units have been combined and now form an internal link from the street to the rear courtyard. This underlines the rising slope of the land which is expressed by several steps and thus gives the terrain on the inside a flowing character. The smaller shop facing towards the road – a hairdressing salon which also commissioned Gerber Architekten with the interior design – benefits especially from the resulting luxurious ceiling height. But the base as a whole is still on just one storey and therefore matches the content and style of the pavilion-like front buildings of the 1960s development to the south, which are also used by retail outlets. This is another link with the local context, avoiding exclusivity and focusing on the urban character of the setting – and thus contrasting with the post-war era which was mainly concerned with fixing and channelling movements and defining exclusive routes. Instead, there are now three different routes by which pedestrians can walk from the station past the RWE Tower towards the market and the pedestrian area, enriching the urban setting in which the RWE Tower plays a moderate guiding role without dominating the setting.

The interior
In spite of its outstanding visual character and the economic importance of its user for Dortmund, the RWE Tower does not aim to be a spectacular solitary building. It is a restrained structure designed for functional use without any air of superiority. This attitude is also evident in the interior, where it forms the basis for functional and aesthetic decisions. First of all, the glass pergola roof in front of the main entrance, which faces Platz von Amiens and thus enhances the urban design, is not an ostentatious gesture, but appears to be systematically developed from the form of the base. The foyer itself, which does not have a windbreak to this outer canopy and is only separated from it by an air curtain, moves around the inner functional core, running parallel to the square and down a few steps. In the original design another shop was to be installed here, but RWE Westfalen-Weser-Ems AG wishes to use the resulting space at the end of the building for exhibitions and similar events. At the same time, the entrance to the central access core and the lifts opens up directly next to the reception desk and through a security sluice door. The black granite of the façade is continued in the reflective floor covering, which contrasts strongly with the white plaster of the walls: this clarity is enhanced by details such as the lack of ceiling girders over the doorways and passages and the round-

ed edges of the lift entrances. In spite of the parallels between the exterior and interior design, the inside is more delicate; this can be seen in the foyer, although some elements of the character of the exterior are also preserved.

Fortunately, the client and RWE Westfalen-Weser-Ems AG also followed Gerber's colour concept, which basically focuses on the restrained elegance of various shades of black, dark grey and white. This corresponds to the reductionist use of materials, and it is characteristic of Gerber's work. A similar colour scheme can be found in the stable building of Dortmund's ›Tönnishof‹, which the architect has converted for use as his own office, and in most of his projects, often with a few contrasting shades of a warmer colour scheme. The ceilings and walls in the RWE Tower are pure white, but anthracite is used for the two small kitchens at the end of the inner core on each storey, the fitted carpets and the steel frames of the glass doors which are coated with translucent film. The milky white of the translucent door coverings is also used for the large glass partitions in the conference and training area on the 20th floor, while RWE Westfalen-Weser-Ems AG decided to use closed partition walls on the normal storeys. Although this restricts the view from the interior corridors more than would be necessary in the flexible and generously partitionable office accommodation, the translucent glass doors nevertheless provide the corridors with daylight so that those can be used without artificial light during the day. Open areas have been created in front of the lifts on the storey used by the management; here and on the conference floor, Gerber was also responsible for the interior design, so he was able to provide furnishings with restrained colours and forms to ensure consistency with the design of the building.

It is against this background, that the architecture and colour scheme form a deliberate and powerful counterpoint on the topmost storey of the building. The spacious canteen was also designed as a coherent whole, including its furnishings and fittings. But the counters of the open kitchen area and the carpet on the wide sweep of the floor and the gallery are designed in a strong orange-red colour. The gallery was designed as a filigree steel structure along the length of the inner core of the building, thus creating a distinct three-dimensional effect in the high semi-circular canteen. The final touch which gives this room an uplifting sensation is the glass roof, which forms the ceiling of the room and provides ample daylight in combination with the tall windows, making the users feel that they are almost outside. The fact that the sloping glass roof reduced the need for extra roof drainage structures also helps to underline the clarity of the atmosphere in the room. Slender supports span the roof and seem to dematerialise where they disappear into the reflective metal sheeting. There are not even any sun protection features to disturb the view, there are simply black dots, invisible to the eye, which are printed on the roof facing north-east. The people in the canteen see nothing but sky and clouds when they look up. And looking through the windows, they can see the breathtaking panorama of the city.

Sustainability as a structural concept
The clear form of the glass roof, which serves to enhance the spatial perception, fits perfectly into Gerber's surprisingly logical and deliberately reductionist treatment of the indoor climate in the building. Naturally this applies even more to the vertical façade and the sophisticated and prudent ecological design used to create a pleasant indoor climate, which largely determines the amount of energy needed to operate the building. In high-rise architecture this topic came into especially sharp focus after the single glazing used in the ›autistic boxes‹ of the 1950s and 1960s made the ›sick building syndrome‹ a widespread problem, while the physical properties of the buildings were ruined by condensation and in some cases even icicles inside the buildings. It is now common knowledge that fully air conditioned buildings are outdated, and that windows which can be individually opened are at least a desirable standard in the construction of tower buildings. But the technological development – and the public perception – have concentrated mainly on achieving these standards by the complex and expensive means in fully transparent tower buildings. The perforated façade of the RWE Tower takes a different approach by considerably reducing the proportion of glass in the façade, and thus providing a building structure which is intrinsically protected against overheating and excessive cooling. The design of the window apertures supports this by exploiting the advantages of a double façade with a ventilated space between the layers. The interior layer has double glazed windows which can be individually opened, while the outer layer consists of a single pane of glass with horizontal slits at the top and bottom. This provides protection against excessive winds when the window is open, and it covers a sun protection blind of metal louvres in the gap which is completely concealed when it is raised. Coated textile sheets inside the rooms serve as protection against glare. The indoor climate can thus be controlled individually and by means of natural ventilation. This system is only augmented at peak times by individual radiators fitted below the windows and a cooling system which provides conditioned air and which activates the properties of the building's concrete core. Two storeys have a chilled ceiling as an alternative system.

In this way, the building achieves a sustainability in the use of energy which is directly reflected, in the everyday use of the building, in a minimised energy consumption at the lower end of the ranges quoted in recent legal ordinances. This strict technological discipline is unusual for a building of this type, but it is a logical conclusion within the overall concept of the tower. Individual factors such as recuperative and regenerative heat recovery, a heating system that is designed for low temperature operation and connected to the district heating grid and the prudent use of the structural materials for thermal storage are not isolated features – instead, they should be considered as functional and interactive elements of the overall design. Like the selection of a perforated façade, which can equally be interpreted as a condition and a consequence of the structural and spatial design, the relationship between the air conditioning system and the structure of the building can also be seen as a coherent whole which increases the spatial quality and flexibility, and at the same time maximises the possibility of individual control with a greatly improved indoor climate. Naturally, the individual decisions in Dortmund also had to take economic feasibility into account because there is a limit to commercial rents and the building was not primarily planned as a showcase for a corporate identity. But instead of treating this as a restriction of his resources for design, the architect responded with a coherent concept which avoids the need for complex façade technology to cure the self-inflicted problems of excessive heating or cooling caused by features such as all-glass façades. The architect Helmut Jahn, who can be regarded as a representative of a highly developed glass architecture, once pointed out that ›the most ecological building in an absolute sense‹ is a building ›which does not need any technical building services at all‹. Of course the RWE Tower is not able to fulfil this high goal. But its focus on the virtues of a ›conservative‹ design which is aware of the qualities of mass and balanced façade openings – and it is very fitting that this concept is demonstrated in the headquarters of an energy and water supply company – is worth serious consideration by proponents of a radical reduction in energy.

Penetration
It is all the more important to note that this does not reflect a dogmatic attitude on the part of the architect. Gerber's office has already produced major designs for all-glass tower buildings – to suit the context and the budget parameters. They include the competition entry for the Twin Towers in Qingdao, China (2003), which was governed by completely different parameters because of the cultural context and the goals of the competition. The decisive basic element is the degree of penetration, the extent to which the detail is consistent with the ›larger whole‹ and requires creative decisions in spite of all pragmatism. This is the factor which creates an unsentimental relationship with the location. One example in the RWE Tower is the fact that the precise external window dimensions in front of the recessed parapet are not based on climatic and structural considerations alone, but follow an aesthetic purpose. It is noticeable, however, that the pattern of vertical rectangular forms in the sober volume of Dortmund's architecture is a familiar timeless theme which recurs in many different buildings such as the ›Stadthaus‹ (a municipal building), the Chamber of Commerce and Industry, the C&A building, the concave façade of the Museum of Art and Cultural History and, last not least, Mario Botta's long rectangular library building. In Botta's case this clearly reflects the ›Stadttheater‹, Dortmund's main city theatre building dating from the 1960s. In fact, the combination of a closed rectangular block and a free glass-clad structure in the library is, as a whole, similar to the composition of the theatre. Gerber's building has nothing to do with this composition, but in a restrained manner and without directly quoting the work of Botta it nevertheless reflects a cautious relationship which is expressed in the curvature of the glossy black façade and the vertical format of the windows. By creating a balanced proportion of open and closed surface areas, he also comes close to the design principle which is apparent in the Harenberg Building, which he also designed. The fact that a square was used as the module for the Harenberg Building only serves to underline this similarity. Eckhard Gerber is naturally not specifically ›interested in‹ one or the other of these formats in the literal sense. The significant factor is the design principle of rationality which creates an almost abstract form in both cases, thus setting each building apart from the city context, although they both interact closely with the surrounding buildings.

The visible differences compared with the Harenberg Building clearly show that it is not the specific individual decisions in the RWE Tower which reflect the fundamental approach in the architect's work, but the principles from which these decisions are derived. In the Harenberg Building, too, Gerber combined a striking structure with a prominent flat form which reverses the relationship of figure and ground by drawing its layout directly from the curved alignment line of the road. The radical orientation towards the station underlines this ›argument‹ and displays a pragmatism in the urban design which appears almost ironical and has a certain similarity with the way the existing supplier entrance ramp is treated by the RWE Tower. The lower part of the Harenberg Building, and especially the glazed intermediate section, has a prestige value which is reflected in the fact that the user makes this part of the building available for cultural events. This public prestige value is absent in the RWE Tower because the necessary programme is not applicable: it is an office building with a base that is partly used for shops. The building provides a splendid setting for this use, but it does not claim to be more, so it conveys a cool and sober impression which is attractive in its own way. Even the elegance of the shining black façade would hardly be conceivable as an end in itself. But it creates a deliberately moderate reflection of the tower against the sky (in contrast with the IWO Tower with its bright mirror-like façade which was renovated in 1991), and the slender effect of the façade gives the building an astonishing sense of lightness. For these reasons, this façade design is essential for the overall impression, i.e. the integration of a building of this size into the city.

Architecture in relation
Finally, the design of the RWE Tower can also be interpreted as a comment on the skyscraper debate that has flared up in Germany every now and then – and which even seems to have a timeless character. Since this type of building was created it has been the subject of public controversy, and sometimes this controversy has been expressed in populist forms. It seems difficult to avoid prejudice because the simple fact that a building rises up high is often interpreted as a symbol of power, especially because many such buildings seem to aim for a spectacular solitary uniqueness. In places such as Munich, where the maximum height has been fixed at 100 metres by a referendum, or in Cologne, where the cathedral was in danger of losing its world cultural heritage status because of plans for high-rise buildings, the discussion is often focused primarily on the city skyline (which is certainly important), sometimes on the lines of sight between landmarks, but it rarely goes any further. Fortunately, superficial arguments like these did not prevail in Dortmund. This was not only because of the architecture of the new skyscraper, which is very modest in height compared with international skyscrapers, but also because of the structure and the development prospects of the city, in which the new building plays a natural symbolic and functional role. The difficulties of structural change, which affected Dortmund all the more because the city was one of the most prosperous places in post-war-Germany, have been largely overcome and can now be seen as an opportunity. When Manfred Sack wrote in the mid-1980s that Dortmund as a city seemed ›always as if its image had not arisen by patient planning over the last three decades, and certainly not with a long-term perspective, but always by rather sudden decisions,‹ this was an accurate observation at that time. Today, however, the most important focal points for development, especially in the city centre, have not only been defined, they have also been linked together by an underlying concept, and this is increasingly reflected in the buildings. And it is worth noting that with only a few exceptions, such as the controversial station project, this development also draws on the recent past instead of breaking with the historical development, as long as this approach can be preserved through to the implementation phase. The sensitive development plans for Kampstrasse by the architects Fritschi Stahl Baum, which are closely linked with Platz von Amiens, are one example of this. At the same time, this development also shows a positive moderation which could often be wished for elsewhere, a restraint which recognises the quality of the traditional character of the city.

The RWE Tower applies this restraint. The building, in which 700 of the 2,700 employees of RWE Westfalen-Weser-Ems AG work, fits in between two existing tower buildings. These three buildings form a group which marks an established administrative location within the city centre. Dortmund's concept for high-rise buildings supplements this area with additional towers at the points where the radial roads leading into the city cross the circular road – like city gates which mark the existing urban structure. The RWE Tower confidently takes its place among the very different contexts and individual buildings in the area – its two older counterparts, the library, the Harenberg Building which it points to, the surrounding streets and open spaces – and in a wider sense forms its functional relationship with cultural and commercial buildings such as the concert hall, the Museum of Art and Cultural History, the station. Because this situation is treated as a specific setting, the design does not offer a universal answer. But it presents a model that is convincingly logical and natural: aesthetic, functional, economically viable, individual in character – a model that especially benefits from a client which is building for its own portfolio and recognises high quality architecture and sustainability as its highest priorities. Respecting the image of the ›European City‹ does not necessarily mean that no skyscrapers should be built. Gerber's building offers a positive contribution here: more than everything else, skyscrapers are buildings which affect the urban context, architecture in relation to other buildings and spaces. This, and not a general principle, is what determines their quality.

Schwarzplan der Dortmunder Innenstadt mit Hauptbahnhof und RWE Tower in zentraler Lage zwischen Wallring und Kampstraße

As-built plan of the city centre of Dortmund with the main station and RWE Tower (centre) between Wallring and Kampstrasse

Rund vier Jahrzehnte nach Errichtung des IWO- und des Sparkasse-Hochhauses ist in deren Mitte der RWE Tower getreten. Vor seiner aufsteigenden Fassade lagern die gläserne Halbrotunde und der steinerne Quader der Stadt- und Landesbibliothek von Mario Botta.

Approximately 40 years after the erection of the IWO and Sparkasse high-rise buildings, the RWE Tower has now been placed alongside them. In front of its rising façade lie the semi-circular glass structure and the rectangular block of the new municipal and regional library designed by Mario Botta.

Fensterflügel und Brüstungen liegen hinter einer rahmenlosen Prallscheibe, die lediglich um die Stärke des schwarzen Granits zurückversetzt wurde. Das rationale Fassadenbild zeichnet die Struktur der Primärkonstruktion nach.

Casements and balustrades are situated behind a frameless full-size window pane which is set back merely by the thickness of the polished black granite. The rational appearance of the façade reflects the building's primary structure.

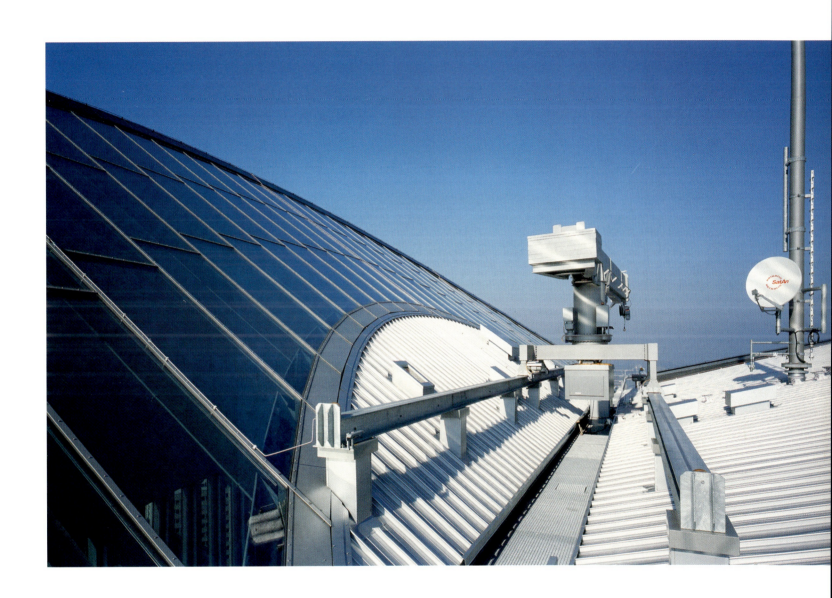

In knapp 100 Metern Höhe überspannt ein geneigtes Glasdach das Kasino im obersten Geschoss.
Die klare »Schnittfläche« stützt den Eindruck, das Gebäude sei aus zwei gebogenen, zueinander gestellten Schalen gefügt.

At a height of nearly 100 metres, a slanted glass roof spans the canteen in the uppermost storey. The clearly
defined ›intersection‹ enhances the impression that the building consists of two arched shells placed next to each other.

Der eingeschossige Sockel löst sich von der geometrischen Form des Baukörpers. Er bindet die Abfahrt zur Tiefgarage ein und reagiert zugleich pragmatisch auf Baurecht und baulichen Kontext.

The single-storey base is set apart from the structure's geometrical form. It integrates the entrance of the underground car park and at the same time responds pragmatically to the requirements of building laws and the built environment.

Vor dem Haupteingang am neuen Platz von Amiens wandelt sich der Sockel zur Pergola mit gläsernem Dach, die auf selbstverständliche Weise ins Innere des Gebäudes führt.

In front of the main entrance facing Platz von Amiens, the base turns into a glass-roofed pergola which naturally leads the visitor to the main entrance.

Im Foyer setzt sich der schwarze Granit der Fassade als spiegelnder Bodenbelag fort. Empfang und Sicherheitsschleuse folgen der reduzierten Formensprache und Farbwahl der Architektur.

Inside the foyer, the black granite of the façade is continued in the reflecting floor covering. The reception desk and security sluice door correspond to the reductionist form and colour of the overall architecture.

Im geschwungenen, bis zu 17 Meter hohen Raum des Kasinos kontrastiert ein kräftiges Orangerot die zurückgenommene Farbgestaltung der Architektur im Ganzen. Auf der Empore befinden sich weitere Sitzbereiche.

The canteen, with its ceiling height of up to 17 metres beneath the curved roof, is dominated by elements in a bright orange-red colour which form a contrast to the restrained colours of the architecture as a whole. There are other seating areas on the gallery.

Von außen ablesbar auch durch die ansteigende Höhe der Fenster, hat der Architekt hinter dem höheren Stirnbogen einen weiten, lichtdurchfluteten Raum geschaffen, der sich im großzügigen Schwung über die gesamte Breite des Gebäudes erstreckt.

As is reflected on the outside by the greater height of the windows, the architect has created a spacious, light-flooded room under the taller roof arch which extends across the whole width of the building.

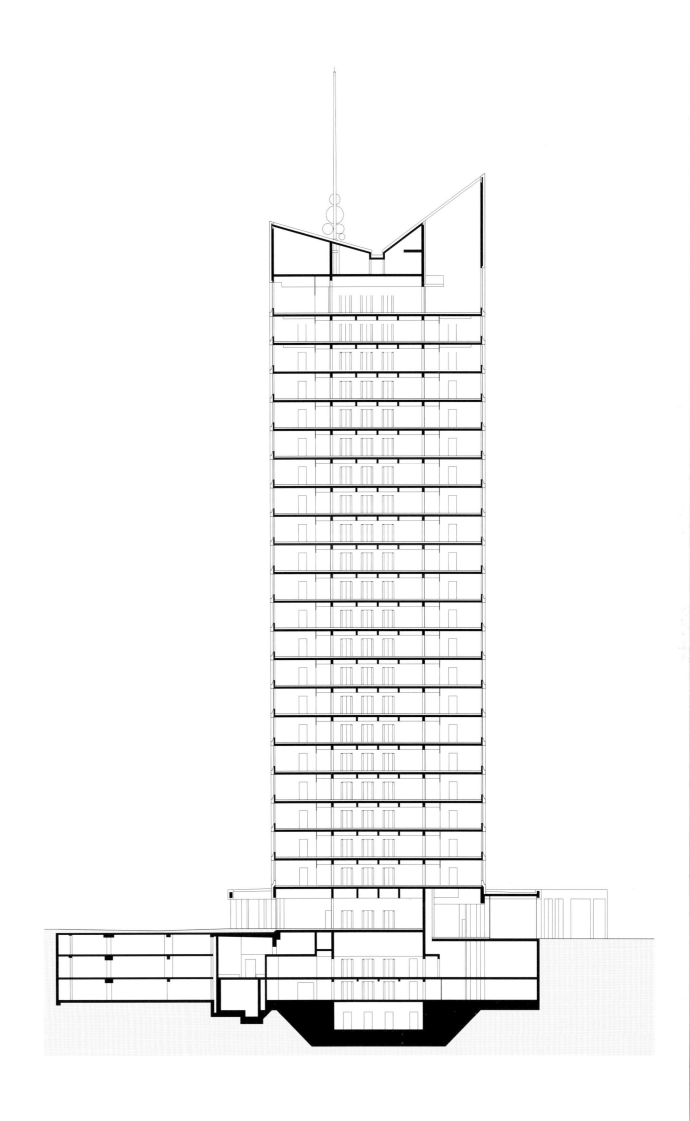

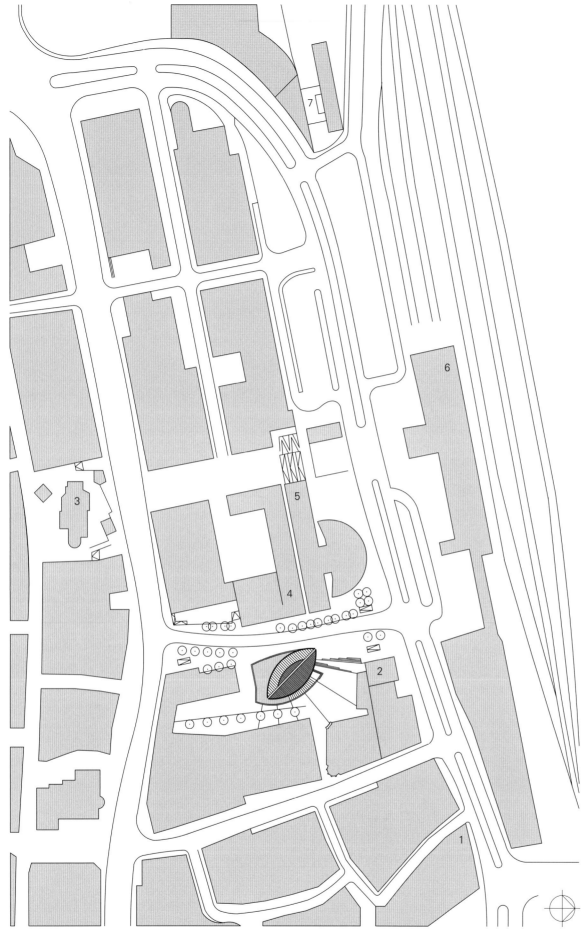

Lageplan (1 Volkshochschule, 2 IWO Hochhaus, 3 Petrikirche, 4 Stadtsparkasse, 5 Stadt- und Landesbibliothek, 6 Hauptbahnhof, 7 Harenberg-Verlag)

Site plan (1 Adult education centre, 2 IWO high-rise building, 3 Petri church, 4 Municipal savings bank, 5 Municipal and regional library, 6 Central station, 7 Harenberg publishing house)

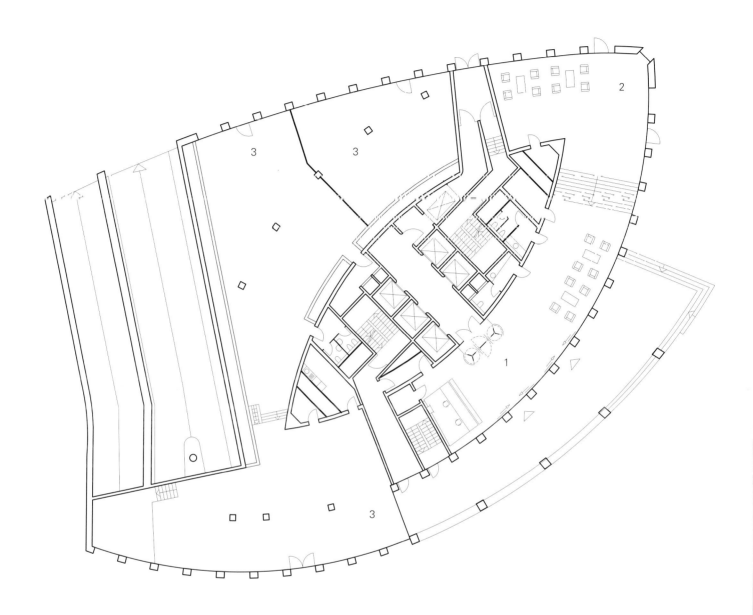

Erdgeschoss (1 Lobby, 2 Foyer/Ausstellung, 3 Laden)

Ground floor (1 Lobby, 2 Foyer/exhibition, 3 Shop)

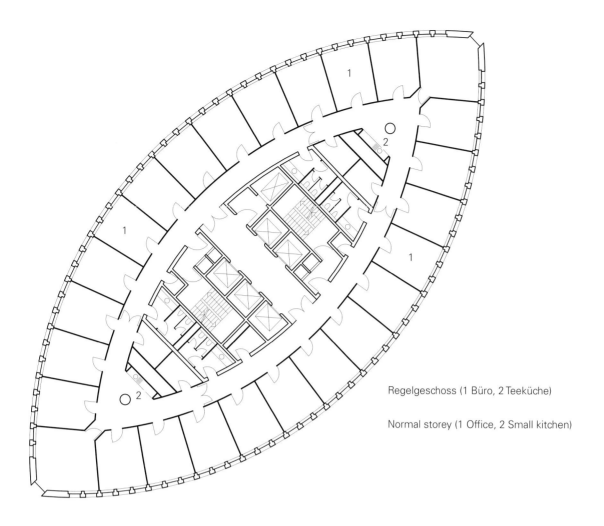

Regelgeschoss (1 Büro, 2 Teeküche)

Normal storey (1 Office, 2 Small kitchen)

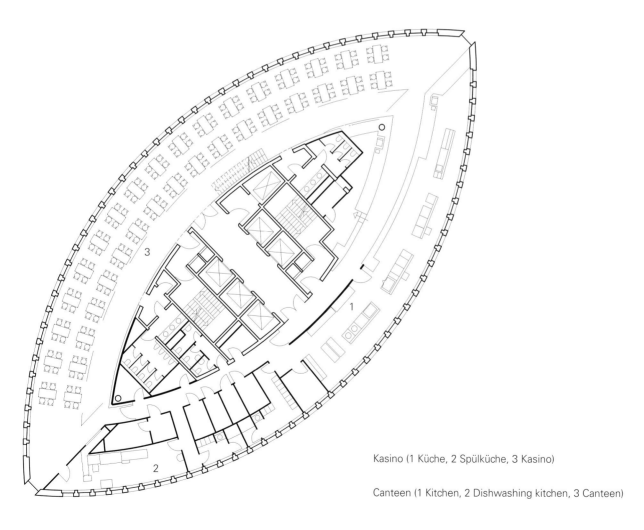

Kasino (1 Küche, 2 Spülküche, 3 Kasino)

Canteen (1 Kitchen, 2 Dishwashing kitchen, 3 Canteen)

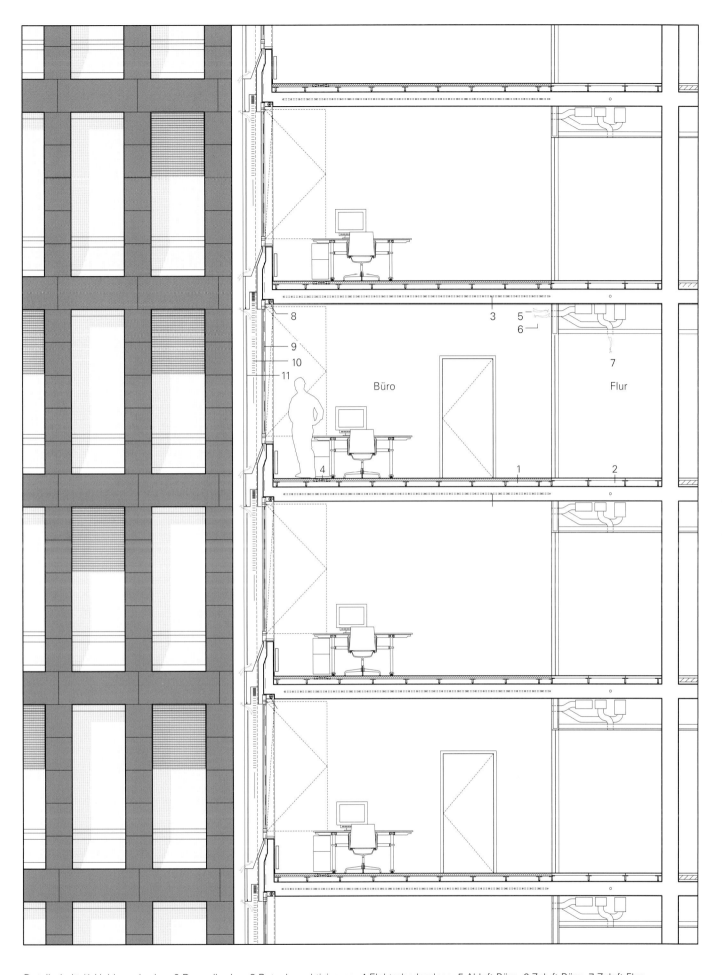

Detailschnitt (1 Hohlraumboden, 2 Doppelboden, 3 Betonkernaktivierung, 4 Elektrobodendose, 5 Abluft Büro, 6 Zuluft Büro, 7 Zuluft Flur, 8 Blendschutz, 9 Wärmeschutz-Isolierverglasung, 10 Sonnenschutz, 11 Prallscheibe VSG)

Detailed cross section (1/2 Cavity floor, 3 Activated concrete core, 4 Electrical floor socket, 5 Air outlet, office, 6 Air intake, office, 7 Air intake, corridor, 8 Facing panel, 9 Thermal insulation glass, 10 Sun protection, 11 Window pane, compound safety glass)

Klarheit und Komplexität
Die Bauten von Professor Eckhard Gerber, Gerber Architekten, Dortmund

Über mehr als drei Jahrzehnte hat Eckhard Gerber im In- und Ausland ein stetig wachsendes, reichhaltiges architektonisches Werk geschaffen. Um diesem weiter nachzuspüren, braucht es vom RWE Tower aus indes nur wenige Schritte. Das Gebäude des Harenberg Verlags (1994) längs der Gleise am Bahnhofsausgang oder das Arbeitsamt (1995) haben die Dortmunder Innenstadt nachhaltig und respektvoll geprägt. Exemplarisch für Gerbers Entwurfshaltung offenbaren sie die Tugenden einer klaren und im besten Sinne zweckmäßigen Architektur: Gerber und seine Mitarbeiter verstehen Architektur auf selbstverständliche Weise als eine Dienstleistung, deren ganzheitliches Gelingen auf dem intensiven und produktiven Austausch zwischen Architekt, Bauherren und Nutzern fußt. Daraus erwachsen Entwürfe, die sich als individuelle Lösungen zu einem konsistenten Werk dauerhafter Bauten fügen.

Die Architektursprache, die Eckhard Gerber in diesen Entwürfen pflegt, ist offensichtlich der klassischen Moderne verpflichtet. Sie erkennt die Qualitäten klarer Geometrien als rationales und zugleich künstlerisches Gestaltungsmittel an, sei es in selbstständiger Existenz oder in differenzierter, komplexer Komposition. Das Detail bindet sich ein in ein Ganzes; die funktionale wie soziale innere Struktur bleibt im Äußeren ablesbar und verbindet sich mit dem sie umgebenden Kontext. Damit zeigt sich zugleich die grundlegende Differenz zu jenem Zug der modernen Architektur, der in Ortlosigkeit mündete: Gerbers Bauten sind Teil jenes Ortes, in den sie sich einfinden und aus dem sie erwachsen.

Dieser positiv verstandene Pragmatismus, der ein formal wie inhaltlich undogmatischer ist, hat sicherlich mit dazu beigetragen, dass sich Gerber Architekten unter anderem als ein erfolgreiches Wettbewerbsbüro verstehen dürfen. Wenige Büros in Deutschland können in dem immer schwieriger werdenden Feld des Wettbewerbswesens stetig über die Jahre auf ein gleichermaßen erfolgreiches Wirken verweisen. Spiegelbild dessen ist, dass Eckhard Gerber seit der Bürogründung in Dortmund im Jahre 1979 und auch schon davor eine umfassende Zahl unterschiedlichster Bauten der öffentlichen Hand realisieren konnte, darunter zahlreiche Universitäts- und Laborbauten wie das Zentralgebäude der Universität Koblenz-Landau, aber auch etwa der Umbau für das Ministerium für Verkehr, Bau- und Wohnungswesen in Berlin. Wie die Messe Karlsruhe, das hochgeschätzte MDR Landesfunkhaus in Magdeburg oder der Konzertsaal der Leipziger Hochschule für Musik und Theater tragen diese Entwürfe zur baulichen Kultur des Landes bei.

Gerber Architekten sind bekennende Generalisten; ihr Verständnis vom Arbeitsfeld des Architekten meint das gesamte Spektrum planerischer Tätigkeit von der Stadtplanung bis zum Innenraum und ebenso die ganzheitliche Herangehensweise an jeden einzelnen dieser Entwürfe. Diese Haltung und die konstitutive Bereitschaft, für alle entwerferischen und wirtschaftlichen Belange hochkomplexer Planungsprozesse umfassende Verantwortung zu übernehmen, haben längst auch zur internationalen Wahrnehmung des Werkes von Gerber Architekten geführt. Zu den Erfolgen im Ausland zählen so bemerkenswerte Wettbewerbsgewinne wie jene für die König Fahad Nationalbibliothek (2002) und für die Prince Salman Science Oasis (2004) in Riad, Saudi-Arabien. Beide Bauten, die nun zur Realisierung anstehen, weisen nach, wie sich planerische Kompetenz und hohes technisches Wissen auch im fremden Kontext bewähren. Voraussetzung dafür ist eine aus Erfahrung gewachsene Architekturphilosophie, die die Gestaltung und Realisierung ästhetisch, ökologisch und ökonomisch nachhaltiger Bauten erlaubt.

Clarity and Complexity
The Work of Professor Eckhard Gerber, Gerber Architekten,
Dortmund/Germany

For more than three decades Eckhard Gerber has created a constantly growing and rich portfolio of architectural work at home and abroad. Only a few steps away from the RWE Tower there are other buildings by Gerber such as the Harenberg Publishing House (1994) along the railway tracks near the station and the employment agency (1995). Both buildings have had a sustained and respectful effect on the city centre of Dortmund. They are typical examples of Gerber's approach to design and show the virtues of an architecture that is clear and functional in the best sense. Gerber and his staff see architecture as a service which achieves all-round success through intensive and productive cooperation with all of their project partners, clients and users. This leads to designs which are individual solutions, but which collectively form a consistent work of enduring buildings.

The architectural forms which Eckhard Gerber uses in his designs are obviously indebted to classical Modernism. They recognise the quality of clear geometry as a rational and yet artistic design feature, both independently and in a more differentiated and complex composition. The details fit into the whole; the functional and social inner structure is revealed by the outside appearance and merges with the surrounding environment. At the same time, this contrasts fundamentally with trends in modern architecture to negate the local settings: Gerber's buildings form part of the situation into which they are placed and from which they develop.

This positive concept of pragmatism, which is non-dogmatic in its form and content, is also one of the factors which have enabled Gerber Architekten to establish themselves successfully in competitions, too. Only a few architects in Germany can look back on an equally successful and consistent track record in competitions. This is reflected by the fact that since the office was founded in Dortmund in 1979, and even before that, Eckhard Gerber has implemented a wide range of very different public sector buildings, including numerous university and research institute buildings – such as the main building of the University of Koblenz-Landau – and the conversion work for the German Ministry of Transport, Building and Housing in Berlin. These buildings, and also the Karlsruhe trade fair complex, the highly acclaimed MDR broadcasting headquarters in Magdeburg and the concert hall of the Leipzig University of Music and Theatre, contribute to the architectural culture of the country.

Eckhard Gerber is a convinced generalist whose architectural concepts cover the whole range of planning activities from urban planning to interior design, and he approaches each single project on a holistic basis. This attitude and his fundamental willingness to assume full responsibility for all design and economic issues which are associated with highly complex planning processes have contributed to the international reputation of Gerber's work. The office's success abroad includes notable competition awards such as the King Fahad National Library (2002) and the Prince Salman Science Oasis (2004) in Riyadh, Saudi Arabia. Both buildings, which are now to be built, prove that planning competence and a high level of technical expertise are the key factors, even in the very special context of a foreign country, especially because they are consistently based on an architectural philosophy which has grown from experience and therefore permits the design and implementation of buildings which are sustainable in their aesthetics and their ecological and economic characteristics.

Niedersächsische Staats- und Universitätsbibliothek/State and University Library of Lower Saxony, Göttingen, 1985-1993.

Harenberg Verlag, Dortmund/Harenberg Publishing House, Dortmund, 1989-1994.

Bundesministerium für Verkehr, Sanierung des Altbaus / Federal Ministry of Transportation, refurbishment of the historic building, Berlin, 1995-1998.

Landesfunkhaus Sachsen-Anhalt des Mitteldeutschen Rundfunks (MDR) / MDR State Office Broadcasting Centre of Saxony-Anhalt, Magdeburg, 1994-1998.

Hauptstelle der Dortmunder Volksbank/Headquarters of the Mutual Savings Bank ›Dortmunder Volksbank‹, Dortmund, 1998-2001.

Konzert- und Theatersaal der Hochschule für Musik und Theater »Felix Mendelssohn Bartholdy«/Concert Hall and Theatre of the University of Music and Theatre ›Felix Mendelssohn Bartholdy‹, Leipzig, 1995-2001.

Zentralgebäude der Universität Koblenz-Landau, Campus Koblenz/Main building of the Koblenz-Landau University, Campus Koblenz, 1997-2001.

Jugendanstalt Raßnitz/Juvenile Detention Centre Raßnitz, 1996-2002.

Chemisches Landes- und Staatliches Veterinäruntersuchungsamt/Chemical State and National Veterinary Research Office, Münster, 2000-2003.

Architekturatelier Tönnishof, Sanierung/Architecture Studio ›Tönnishof‹, refurbishment, Dortmund, 2000-2003.

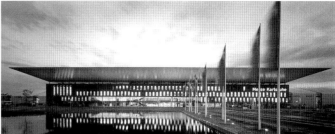

Neue Messe / New Exhibition Grounds, Karlsruhe, 2000-2003.

Biologische Institute der Technischen Universität Dresden / Institutes for Biological Research of the Dresden University, 2001-2005.

Projektdaten / Project data

Planungsbeginn	Januar 2003
Baubeginn	September 2003
Fertigstellung	30. Juni 2005
Tiefgarage	
Stellplätze	361
Bruttorauminhalt	25.500 m²
Bürogebäude	
vermietbare Fläche	22.150 m²
Bruttogrundrissfläche	27.300 m²
Bruttorauminhalt	103.000 m³
Fassadenfläche gesamt	11.200 m²
Fensterfläche	4.500 m²
geschlossene Außenfassade	6.700 m²

Start of Planning	January 2003
Start of Construction	September 2003
Completion	30 June 2005
Underground car park	
Parking spaces	361
Gross cubic volume	25,500 m³
Office building	
Rentable floor space	22,150 m²
Gross floor space	27,300 m²
Gross cubic volume	103,000 m³
Total façade area	11,200 m²
Windows	4,500 m²
Solid exterior façade	6,700 m²

Bauherr / Client
DIAG GmbH & Co. KG II,
44141 Dortmund

Bauherrenberater / Client's consultant
Architekt Nikolai Jürgensen,
45133 Essen

Nutzer (Mieter) / User (tenant)
RWE Westfalen-Weser-Ems AG,
44139 Dortmund

Architekt / Architect
Gerber Architekten
44149 Dortmund

Projektteam / Project team
Prof. Eckhard Gerber
Projektdirektor / Project director: Jens Haake
Projektleiter / Project manager: Rolf Knie
Mitarbeiter / Employees:
Hans-Christoph Bittner
Andrzej Bleszynski
Juana Grunwald
Birgit Hassenteufel
Holger Heltewig
Susanne Kreimeyer
Nils Kummer
Petra Luis
Markus Petry
Simone Saul
Jörg Schoeneweiß
Keith Stoltenfeldt
Martin Timmermann

Planungsbeteiligte / Project Participants

Projektsteuerung, Bauleitung, Kostenkontrolle
Project management, site supervision, cost monitoring
Gerber Architekten
44149 Dortmund

Planung Außenanlagen
Planning of outdoor facilities
Gerber Architekten
44149 Dortmund

Entwurfsberatung Tragwerk
Design consultant for the load-bearing structure
Prof. Pfeifer und Partner
Ingenieurbüro für Tragwerksplanung
64285 Darmstadt

Tragwerksplanung
Planning of the load-bearing structure
IB Düffel – Ingenieurgesellschaft für Tragwerksplanung mbH
44287 Dortmund

Elektroplanung
Electrical planning
Kleinmann Engineering
Ing.-Gesellschaft für techn. Gebäudeausrüstung mbH
44143 Dortmund

Haustechnische Planung
Planning of building services:
HL Technik AG
81379 München

Ingenieurbüro Fuhrmann & Keuthen
Technische Gebäudeausrüstung
47533 Kleve

Bauphysik / Akustik
Construction physics / acoustics
Ingenieurbüro Henrich
44793 Bochum

Fassadenberatung / Façade consulting
AMP – Ingenieurbüro für
Fassadentechnik und angewandte Bauphysik GbR
41470 Neuss

Küchenplanung / Kitchen planning
IBS & Partner
06618 Naumburg

SiGeKo
Health and safety coordinator
AGS Weckermann & Partner
44141 Dortmund

Vermesser / Surveyor
Öffentl. best. Verm.-Ingenieur
Dipl.-Ing. Christian Sommerhoff
44229 Dortmund

Prüfstatiker
Inspecting structural engineer
Ingenieursozietät
Schürmann-Kindmann und Partner GbR
44269 Dortmund

Bodengutachter / Soil engineer
EA Herdecke
Ing.-Gesellschaft für Geotechnik und Umwelt
58313 Herdecke

Brandschutzgutachter
Independent fire protection expert
Sachverständigenbüro Halfkann + Kirchner
41812 Erkelenz

Lichtkunst / Lighting art
LichtVision GmbH
10777 Berlin

Vita Eckhard Gerber

1938	Geboren in Oberhain, Thüringen	1938	Born in Oberhain, Thuringia
1959-1966	Architekturstudium an der Technischen Hochschule Braunschweig; Stipendiat des Begabtenförderungswerks der Firma Reemtsma, Hamburg	1959-1966	Studied Architecture at the Technical University of Brunswick; grant from the Reemtsma Scholarship Fund, Hamburg
1966	Gründung des Büros »Werkgemeinschaft 66«	1966	Founded the studio »Werkgemeinschaft 66«
1973-1975	Assistent an der Universität Dortmund am Lehrstuhl Professor Harald Deilmann	1973-1975	Assistant at the University of Dortmund under Professor Harald Deilmann
1975	Förderpreis für junge Künstler des Landes Nordrhein-Westfalen für das Jahr 1974 auf dem Gebiet Städtebau und Architektur	1975	Award for Young Artists from the federal state of North Rhine-Westphalia for 1974 in City-Planning and Architecture
seit 1979	Gerber Architekten, Dortmund; erfolgreiche Wettbewerbe im In- und Ausland, zahlreiche Auszeichnungen für die realisierten Bauten	since 1979	Gerber Architekten, Dortmund; successful competition entries in Germany and in other countries, numerous prizes for realized buildings
1981-1992	Professur an der Universität-Gesamthochschule Essen, Lehrgebiet Grundlagen der Gestaltung und angewandte Gestaltungslehre für Architektur und Landespflege	1981-1992	Professor of Design Basics and Applied Theory of Design in Architecture and Regional planning at the University of Essen
1990-2004	Professur an der Bergischen Universität Wuppertal, Lehrgebiet Grundlagen des Entwerfens und Entwerfen für Architektur	1990-2004	Professor of Design Basics and Design in Architecture at the University of Wuppertal
seit 1992	Vorsitzender des Dortmunder Kunstvereins	since 1992	Chairman of the Dortmund Art Association
1995-1999	Dekan des Fachbereichs Architektur der Bergischen Universität Wuppertal	1995-1999	Dean of the Department of Architecture at the University of Wuppertal
	Mitglied im BDA, DWB, Vielfache Tätigkeit als Juryvorsitzender bei Architekturwettbewerben, Vortragstätigkeit im In- und Ausland		Member of the BDA, DWB, frequently head of the jury in architectural competitions, speaker on conferences in Germany and abroad
seit 2004	Professur an der Bergischen Universität Wuppertal im Masterstudiengang REM & CPM, Lehrgebiet Grundlagen des Entwerfens und Entwerfen für Architektur	since 2004	Professor of Design Basics and Design in Architecture in the Master's Study Course in REM & CPM at the University of Wuppertal

Junius Verlag GmbH
Stresemannstraße 375
22761 Hamburg
www.junius-verlag.de

Copyright 2006 by Junius Verlag GmbH
Copyright für Fotos, Zeichnungen und Texte:
bei den Fotografen, den Architekten und beim Autor
Alle Rechte vorbehalten

Redaktion: Martina Afken, Jörg Stumpf
Gestaltung: www.qart.de
Satz: Junius Verlag GmbH
Übersetzung: Victor Dewsbery, Berlin

Druckvorstufe, Druck und Bindung:
Druckhaus Dresden GmbH, Dresden

Printed in Germany
ISBN-10 3-88506-565-7
ISBN-13 978-3-88506-565-4
1. Auflage 2006

Bibliografische Information der Deutschen Nationalbibliothek:
Die Deutsche Nationalbibliothek verzeichnet diese Publikation in der Deutschen
Nationalbibliografie; detaillierte bibliografische Daten sind im Internet
über http://dnb.ddb.de abrufbar.

Abbildungen/Copyright notice
S. 6, 13: Hans Jürgen Landes
S. 19: Schwarzplan: Mit freundlicher Genehmigung der Stadt Dortmund/
Katasteramt/With the kind permission of the City of Dortmund/Land Registry;
Luftbild: Hans Blossey, Hamm
S. 20-62: Hans Jürgen Landes
S. 70: oben links und unten: Christian Richters; oben rechts: Peter Walser
S. 71: oben: Linus Lintner; unten: Hans Jürgen Landes
S. 72-74: Hans Jürgen Landes
S. 75 oben rechts: Hans Jürgen Landes; oben links: Archiv Gerber Architekten;
unten: Holger Stein
S. 79: David Klammer, Köln